Feels like Daisy!

Daizy Shekhawat

BookLeaf Publishing

India | USA | UK

Presentation by *BookLeaf Publishing*

Web: www.bookleafpub.com

E-mail: info@bookleafpub.com

ISBN: 9789363311169

First edition 2024

This book and one of the poems is dedicated to Studio Lev, a place that became my sanctuary during moments of doubt and lack of motivation. The warmth and creativity of its community lifted my spirits and reignited my passion for poetry. I extend my heartfelt thanks to Svenja with Amber and Ru, Mi Amore Aurora, Leo, Nora, Marten, Sarah, Almut, Hanna, Toni, Chrisi, Franzi, Norina, and all the wonderful souls I had the pleasure of meeting there. Your friendship and encouragement have been invaluable to me, and I'm forever grateful for the memories and inspiration you've given me.

ACKNOWLEDGEMENT

To my beloved Mumma and Papa, thank you for nurturing my capabilities and allowing me to gather experiences that now find expression in my poetry. To my dear baby brother Ani, your belief in me and constant motivation drive me to strive for excellence every day.

A special appreciation goes to my esteemed Principal Mam Sasmita Mohanty, whose guidance and mentorship have polished me into the jewel I am today. Your enduring influence will always have my utmost gratitude.

My friends hold a significant place in my heart, and I owe much of my experiences to them. I am especially grateful to my dear friend Jarryd D'Abreo, whose encouragement and daily check-ins inspired me to write poetry consistently. Without you, dear Jg, this journey wouldn't have been possible.

Dr. Vandana and Sanskar, Nitesh and Naman my best friends and safe haven, deserves a special mention for their unwavering support and belief in my potential.

To every friend I've made in the past year
Nikhil, Saee, Aboli, Disha, Sheetal you have all
played a vital role in shaping me into the person
I am today. Your presence in my life is cherished
deeply, and you will always hold a special place
in my heart.

A heartfelt thank you to my newfound family in
Germany – My German Mom, Nicole; Dad,
Hans; dearest Andrea and Lotta; and my
wonderful colleagues at the school, including
Hetty, Nicolas, Birgit, Fr. Tidow, Fr. Annacker,
Heike, Bernhard , the most beautiful Franzi , my
bookworm roommate Laura and everyone else.
Your warmth and acceptance have made my
time in Germany truly memorable.

Lastly, a note of appreciation to Instagram,
through which I discovered Book Leaf
Publishing. Thank you for helping me realize
my dream and constantly encouraging and
giving tips on writing via Emails. I am proud
and grateful for taking up the challenge and
seeing it through to completion.

PREFACE

Welcome to my world of poetry. As you turn the pages of this book, I invite you to embark on a journey through the landscapes of my heart and mind.

In crafting this collection, I drew inspiration from my experiences, both near and far. From the cobblestone streets of Germany to the quiet corners of my imagination, each poem is a reflection of moments cherished and emotions felt deeply.

Through these verses, I explore themes of love, longing, and the beauty of the human spirit. Each poem is a testament to the power of words to capture the essence of life and evoke emotion in the reader.

As you delve into these pages, I hope you find solace, inspiration, and a renewed appreciation for the magic of poetry. Thank you for joining me on this poetic journey.

With Warmest Regards,
Daisy.

A Summer Like This.

A white floral Dress
a daisy crochet bag in hand,
a glass of wine
and a paint brush little damped.

sitting on the faint noises of Grass
Along the river side,
with the Sun kissing your ass
a hat and white sunglasses matching your vibe.

A beer in one hand
in another you have fries,
skinny dipping is all you need
if your soul feels heavy and dried.

For summer is known to be a sexy season,
to wear a bikini you'd always have a reason
wet bodies and tanned lines,
full of soul and a sexy mind.

Spring the season one more time.

Spring the season one more time
Let the flowers bloom,
Look at how beautifully the sun shines
No room left for gloom.

Spring the season one more time
For it's called the season of life,
Rain showers everywhere
Restored vigor to thrive.

Spring the season one more time
Where you can live it all ,
From watching the trees turn green
To walking on the leaves from last fall.

Spring the season one more time
Some days hot some cold,
It's the arrival of milder weather
With new lives being unfold.

Tis Autumn.

Tis Autumn
the season of fall,
Apples, Nuts, Squirrels everywhere,
the season i love of them all.

Tis Autumn
look at how beautifully the nature changes color,
shades of brown, orange, green
looks like the earth unites with its lover.

Tis Autumn
the season of pumpkin spice and everything
nice,
orange becomes the new black
and the city covered with spooky lights.

Tis Autumn
kids around the city with tiny Lanterns,
warm cup of coffees and early nights
reminds me of the city whose memories my
heart retains.

I winter sometimes.

I wonder why its called the winter wonderland,
maybe because wonders happen during this
season
the spirit of magic,
just might be one of the reason.

I wonder why its called the season of hope,
in spite of still days and darker nights
the light within peoples heart
overcomes the days of cold.

Its definitely the season of Holiday,
sweets and buttery food is hard to keep away
the season of warm socks and hats
bed snuggles and Glühwein is now happening
everyday.

Diwali, Christmas, New years
the season that brings in so many cheers
no wonder its the season of fairytale,
snow everywhere, shifting life to a cozy gear.

A love letter to my 'Jijosa'.

Weird how life
suddenly changes its gears,
the person you never thought about,
in a moment just disappears.

Weird how you never know
your last call was actually "The last call",
and all you do is wonder
where did this person actually go?

The plans you look forward to,
All the dreams you see together,
Everything just paused as it is
and you stop believing in forever.

That piece of a perfect puzzle is lost,
and a part of you is forever broken,
and you'd never imagine but its worse,
than your childhood teddy being stolen.

And now you go through the worst feeling,
the feeling that you don't understand.
So much hurt, grief, somber and anger,
having no idea if there's a scope of healing.

But then you console yourself,
looking at the enriched life they lived,
so much love and laughter throughout
makes your heart relieved.

Now all you can do is
stay strong and walk on the path of healing,
for the memories they left behind
you'll always have and in life start believing.

Now and then.

Sometimes a five minute spark
leaves you with life long energy,
and sometimes
the energy you put all your life in,
fails to create a spark at all.

The fact that you might never see each other
again,
might be the reason to pour your heart out.
and sometimes,
You hesitate to show the same affection,
because you don't know if you'd ever see them
again.

You create the best memories,
during a limited time.
Then why is it that you don't respect it,
when you know that you have all life.

This is the nature of life,
On the other side the grass is always green.
it takes ages to learn,
it's actually where you water it the most,
you know what i mean.

Kassel!

Writing this poem
so that i can come back to it when i feel lost,
it's about a city
which i love the most.

The once in 5 years Documenta!
and the incredible statue of Hercules!
I don't know what's more famous,
The Kassel honey or its bees!

It's a tiny city
with a very great history
was considered to be the capital once
but then the idea became Valedictory.

The home to the famous "Wolfsheim"
and the opulent Bergpark!
the mesmerizing city lights view
Feels like "Märchenhaft" on the days of dark.

Starry skies, breathtaking sunsets,
and the fragrance of lavender everywhere,
when you love going on mindful walks
of kassel Waschbare you've to be aware.

I fell in love with myself,
Because of all i learned from this city.
The courage of getting out
never made me feel so pretty.

The most precious part of the city,
are the people i found,
A huge piece of my heart now resides there,
It's the steeple resound.

oh! and to stop writing about it
is a task little hard,
not a single day passes by
without humming "Kassel ist ein schöne
stadt...".

My Kinda Love.

Not just one but ten texts
that make your day kinda love,
Meeting them always feels like
soft butterfly kisses kinda love.

Let me buy you flowers everyday
and a present when we go on dates,
you make me feel radiant
every time we meet, kinda love.

Let's talk about our dreams,
Go on long romantic walks
Let weird and crazy be our love language
and embrace the sanity, kinda love.

Talk about things that feel uncomfortable,
and create a safe space to be vulnerable,
A bubble to hide in when you don't want to face
the world,
"Don't worry i got you" kinda love.

Dancing to Jazz music while cooking,
Giving each other sugared kisses when no one's
looking,
Princess twirls in the moments of bliss,
Bear hugs on sad days, kinda love.

Unbound by the constraints of Gender,
Dancing in the feelings of love so tender,
Nothing's sexier than entwining responsibilities,
"Fly me to the Moon" kinda love.

OMG my parents are insanely in love
kinda love,
"Aren't you guys old to do that?"
kinda love,
Let's build a house in the forests
kinda love,
let's travel the world together
kinda love,
i love your silence
kinda love,
Honey! I cherish you everyday
kinda love.

Nature's Child.

I am the child of the forest
but i am stuck in city dust,
playing with all the plants,
helps get out the inner rust.

I am the child of water
But i am stuck within these borders,
imagine rivers as clean as your pool
now wouldn't that be cool?

I am the child of the fire
but i am stuck in a social mire,
want to burn them all
and then suddenly disappear.

I am the child of the air,
but i am always compared
to the affluent friends
yet i never seem to care.

I'd rather dance in the rain
or jump in a puddle
open my arms to hug a tree
and with the mountain winds cuddle.

It's time to give back what we used
at the end it's our planet
this fact let's not loose
let us all save it together!

A small town girl.

a small town girl,
Who's stuck between two worlds
Doesn't know which one to choose
And is worried that something she'll lose.

One is where she was born,
Learned about life ,
Has childhood friends and family,
The one with the best of the times!

Another is where she learned to live,
Felt that she always belonged there,
The things she only dreamt of ,
To live that she'd finally dare.

a small town girl ,
Now can't decide what she wants,
Often wonders, why choose?
Why can't I have it all?

But at the end of the day,
Wherever she stays ,
She'll fill that place with her magic ,
Afterall, she was born to slay.

A better place.

Let's make the world a better place,
We're all running into the rat race instead,
Materialistic things are your greatest possession,
Highest number of followers is the only
Obsession.

Quality time is now with a phone,
Can't find time for yourself to hone,
Instead of moving at a nimble pace
Let's slow down and make the world a better
place.

Let the borders divide us only on Maps,
And not anymore in our hearts,
The misconstrue of inequality and prejudice
Are the prime catalyst that tore us apart .

Let's compete over which country
Is the most peaceful of them all,
The language of love and peace will always
Bring us together we should recall.

Extricating poverty ,racism and
Saving yourself from the dystopic race,
Should now be your soul's sole quest
Only then, would our world be a better place.

Second Chances

The first Kiss after a heart break,
The courage you gather to go on a date
You deserve so much better my love
Is what the Universe tries to say.

Dressing up for yourself,
In your room again you start to Dance
Life happens the best to you,
When you always believe in giving yourself a
chance.

When the soul feels fuller than your stomach,
And heart lighter than balloon,
With life you start to catch up
And like a goddess you start to bloom.

The feeling of finding your charm again,
And the wowing at first glance ,
Life happens best to you,
When you always believe in giving yourself a
chance.

Little things.

A baby holding your finger,
be it any age "kala tikka " to save you from evils
eye,
new erasers on the days of exam,
and friends with hard goodbyes.

Mumma's feeding you all day,
and to papa your favorite fruit dare you say,
late night snacking with your brother,
motivation on days you cant move any further.

A tiny habit that,
someone remembers about you,
your cousins assuring you're surrounded
by worries very few.

Forehead kisses every time we meet,
your lover admiring the way people you greet,
Life is all about these little things ,
and these little things are what makes a life.

My jungle Zion.

A dog faced human,
that gives you the best hugs,
an Ant that seeks your help,
for a war between them and the bugs.

A green eyed cat,
trying to make you dance,
your two tiny pet turtles whom you lost,
you're dying to get a glance.

The pandas are the ones,
you most had fun with,
The "Moto Moto" hippo is actually hot,
apart from its scary teeth.

And all in my weird dreams,
I am always "Alex" the lion,
I love to visit them in my dream weaver,
it feels like i am in my Jungle zion.

My Little Krishna.

Declared Mighty before his birth's first morn,
Yet seven siblings' loss, for whom parents
mourned.
Wonders began as he graced this earthly sphere,
Cradled in a basket, through river's depths clear.

Child of two mothers, one birthed, one raised,
Endearing to all, "Makhan" his name praised.
 Eyes like lotus petals, hair a curly cascade,
His flute's melody, villagers' hearts swayed.

In every Indian mother's dreams, he's found,
His tales narrated, with love profound.
Chanting "Hare Ram, Hare Krishna," divine
hymn,
Richer than gems, souls dance with him.

From the womb of adversity, emerged so bright,
 His radiance dispelled the darkest night.
Each step a miracle, each word a sacred verse,
Healing wounds, lifting spirits, a universe

Laughter Realm

Imagine a tiny world of Miniatures, so small,
Living among us, unseen by all.
Déjà vu moments are their tales,
From their world where laughter never fails.

No currency here but laughter's embrace,
A "Lol" buys a meal, a "Rofl", divine grace.
Amidst sorrows, they strive to spread cheer,
Turning tears to smiles, erasing all fear.

Humor is their lifeline, their daily bread,
Their joy spreads, in colors bright and red.
Their happiness, maybe it's the source,
Of all our laughter, a natural force.

When I'm stressed, I close my eyes to see,
The Miniatures' world, where soul shines free,
Living their perfect life, so small yet grand,
In a world where laughter's the only command.

Museum Der Bedeutung.

From "Nichts" came an idea bright,
A museum of meaning, our guiding light.
In "Museum der Bedeutung" we collected tales,
Of tiny things that made life's sails.

A nose ring or the world's vast scope,
Each held value, gave people hope.
Some found joy in possessions held close,
While others shed what didn't impose.

Conversations flowed, sincere and true,
Revealing how small things make life anew.
Yet at the book's end, we're left to see,
Is anything important, or just what we decree?

Satisfiers and turn-offs, we discovered too,
 Adding depth to the stories, old and new.
For some, a precious possession brought delight,
 While others found freedom in shedding what
didn't feel right.

Building the museum was a labor of love,
With researchers donning yellow, like sunshine
above.
With pixel fonts and a wagon to roam,
We captured stories, making each one home.

The Museum of Meaning, a treasure trove,
 Holding love and life, stories to behove.
As we ponder the book's question, we adhere,
Is anything truly important, or just what we hold
dear?

My Kin Buddies.

While friends may come and go, the bond
remains,
But what of cousins, our constant companions in
life's lanes?
Often overlooked, yet always by our side,
In their presence, our joys and sorrows abide.

From vacations to weddings, they're always
there,
Growing together, a bond beyond compare.
We laugh, we tease, we share our woes,
United against parents' scolding, as history
shows.

From dating advice to protective care,
They're always there, ready to share.
Blessed with cousins so dear and true,
Our journey together, forever anew.

From game strategies to life's twists,
Through it all, our bond persists.
No matter where life's path may bend,
Cousins remain, our eternal friend.

A blend of best friends and Parent's embrace,
Cousins, our constants, in life's race.

A love letter to my Guiding Stars.

This is a love letter,
To the ones who truly matter,
The Man I seek in every lover,
And the Woman, whose love is purer than any
other.

This is a love letter to,
My Papa and Mumma,
I am like an egg in their hands,
Strong on the outside, shielded by their loving
strands.

Papa taught me to be strong,
Treats me like his elder son,
But in our safe space, where we belong,
He treats me like a princess, second to none.

Mumma is my best friend,
My tenderness and jokes stem from her,
I'm so grateful to be her daughter,
How she does it all, I always wonder.

"I love you, Maa and Papa,"
Is just a drop in the ocean of my love for you.
Thank you for the values you've bestowed,
And for my baby brother, the best gift I've ever
known.

It's all because of you that I am today,
Your sleepless nights and tireless care,
I'll strive to repay you someday
By being the best daughter, beyond compare.

When Time Pauses.

I often ponder a question these days,
About the most difficult phase:
Our lives filled with endless waiting,
How do we embrace it without hesitating?

The result of an exam we strive to ace,
The answer to a proposal's case,
The job we've wanted for so long,
Or a baby's gender, what could go wrong?

Expectation might bring us sorrow,
But anticipation can shape tomorrow.
We shouldn't give waiting so much weight,
For what's meant for us will never be late.

Learn to embrace and find joy in the wait,
This phase of life need not frustrate.
With patience, life becomes light as a feather,
For effort matters more than results altogether.

Culture Collage.

A year where I landed in a new country,
To work with the most special humans ,
Having no idea how it would end up,
For what was to come next was a indo german
fusion.

Living with most adorable roommates,
Both national and International,
I had no clue I would find my " Main squeeze"
Being it so Unintentional.

And about the kids I worked with,
I can't stop talking,
I had more to learn than to teach,
They made me laugh my heart out on the days I
was sobbing.

I made a new family,
Found warmth in a cold country,
Felt so special to be recognized at their family
gatherings,
So much love, we forgot to set boundaries.

I travelled so much to so many different
countries,
So many people I befriended,
And so many experiences I lived
Made a life I intended.

Living in a different country in one thing,
And belonging there is another,
A part of my heart I left it back there,
I am a girl who's soul is now in two different
worlds divided.